AF488379

What Now?!
Puppy Haiku / Dog Haiku

by Melissa S. Anderson

Production by Patti Frazee

Cover photos by Melissa S. Anderson (top)
and Dan Baldwin (bottom)

Dog footprint: Freepik.com

ISBNs: 979-8-9853117-2-3 (print book)
        979-8-9853117-3-0 (ebook)

Published by
Poppy Anna Press
4629 Abbott Ave. S.
Minneapolis, MN 55410

Author's Website:

mandwriter.com

To Poppy

Table of Contents

Puppy

Haiku

puppy snoozes
in a blankie
all the way home

I play recording
of puppy's howls — friend says,
must have been a loooong night

I hug her,
she licks my face —
puppy love

a house transformed —
gates, toys, blankets,
newspaper all over the floor

little pup
gets lost
in the long grass

puppy
with snootful
of dandelion pollen

how many ways
to get in trouble
within five minutes of waking?

towels
awkwardly placed,
out of puppy's reach

out in public
with smears of slobber
on my jeans

ouch
another puppy tooth
on the floor

her toy against our shins
as we walk down the hall
bonk bonk bonk bonk bonk

outside at 2 a.m.
in mid-January:
Go pee! Go pee!

I sneeze —
pup looks at me
as if I've exploded

pup lies with head on the top step
looking down at me
forlornly

hard for teething pup
to get affection she craves
with all that biting

puppy
is fascinated
by my coffee breath

pup tracks an airplane
across the sky
for the first time

new Lamb Chop toy,
bloody —
more puppy teeth have come out

puppy outside
on a wet day
in her bright yellow raincoat

it's the second time
you try to put on the raincoat
that is hard

quiet morning —
sound of a squeaky toy —
puppy is up

puppy learns fast:
a toe tap on the floor
shows where food is

no, let's not chew
the furniture
today

when, oh when
will this dog
lose her obsession with towels?

after a long walk,
puppy bounds inside
and pees

why is eating
small stones
even a thing?

first grooming —
she is
so tiny!

halfway down the stairs,
she can't figure out
how to turn around

the days of our eating anything
unobserved
are over

twelve teeth gone —
she looks like Bumble
in *Rudolph the Red-Nosed Reindeer*

furious digging
on linoleum floor
gets her nowhere

puppy learns physics:
put on the brakes
or run into the wall

nose-to-nose love fest
with her reflection
on the stove

weather stripping, metal chair,
plastic tarp, rocks —
why are these fun to gnaw?

long welts on my legs —
time to get
her toenails clipped

puppy runs down the hall —
ears flying,
bottom bouncing

today
she decides
to gnaw the stove

sneezes, burps, snorts, sighs —
so adorable
in a puppy

no amount of pawing
will release ice cubes
from the fridge

favorite person arrives —
wiggle! wiggle!
oops, she springs a leak

puppy dawdles
at bedtime,
like any toddler

toilet paper unspooled
down hallway, across kitchen,
to the back door

she scrambles
to get traction on smooth floor —
natural comedian

pup, do you know anything
about the bra
on the kitchen floor?

blessings
on those who make
chew sticks

she barks at
whatever is there,
including the air

tug on the pantleg:
"slow down!
look at me!"

love you,
but I draw the line
at structural damage to the house

wild pulling
on the leash —
my aching shoulders!

puppy —
ecstatic wiggling
for no discernable reason

she trains us how to train her —
yummy treats work,
No does not

bald eagle notices
little puppy,
get out of here!

aww, puppy's sweet little gnaw marks
here and here and
here and here and....

in class, she's thrilled
to see the other dogs,
ignores the teacher

she's quiet,
then lunges for the TP
and runs

wonders on today's walk:
lawn sprinkler, flying bug,
plastic box, dried worm

etiquette lesson:
we don't bark at our friends,
joyous wiggling is fine

she lies on my foot
at the computer — how nice! —
for seven seconds

poor baby,
vaccinations today —
you look miserable

our hands sting
from all the nips
and bites

morning routine:
we fix breakfast,
she pulls toilet paper

she has
the cutest snout
in the whole family

pup lullaby:
tummy wub, tummy wub,
tummy tummy tummy wub

taking dirty pup
into the lake
does not improve things

an empty water bottle
turns puppy
into a wild animal

hot day on the path —
puppy lunges
from shady spot to shady spot

sometimes the cycle —
Drop It, reward, *Drop It*, reward —
feels like blackmail

I bend down to her face
to emphasize *No* —
she just sniffs my breath

bark! bark! bark! bark! bark!
geez!
bark! bark! bark! bark! bark!

long, floppy ears —
it's hard for pup to know
where sound is coming from

digging on the couch —
working on
a portal to China

laser focus of pup
waiting for popcorn
to fall on the floor

the bigger the stick
the happier the pup —
look at her strut!

obedience school dropout:
no interest in
staying on the mat

in the morning
pup races to find me,
careening around corners

my steady pace,
her lunge/stall/lunge/stall —
it all averages out

puppy eats
the dead June bug
whole

she catches the ball
on a bounce for the first time
yay!

puppy is a PR pro —
knows how to get
anyone's attention

puppy
chasing butterfly
in the flower bed

she nudges our ankles
with toys —
"let's play! let's play! let's play!"

puppy obeys *Wait*!
better than
many motorists do

large dog breaks free of small boy,
I grab its collar —
my puppy cowers

groomer tries
to trim her face —
it does not go well

how long until
she finds the world boring enough
to walk briskly?

weeds dangle from her mouth —
she doesn't care
how silly she looks

old license plate, clamp, wire —
contraption to keep her
from pulling TP

tiny white triangles in the grass —
she noses them —
they fly away!

when things are quiet,
we check
to see what she's doing

warm puppy
snoozing
on my tummy

people without dogs
don't know the benefits
of pre-chewed underwear

puppy stops
at every tree
to check peemail

puppy
in the bathtub —
so pitiful!

hot pepper on TP,
with sign for humans: Don't Use —
pup chews the sign

how long
until scrambling into the car
is replaced by graceful leaps?

pup grabs a clod of sod
and carries it
for half a mile

twitching ears, nose, legs
and a soft bark —
puppy dreaming

yeah! bark at those leaves
so they'll stop blowing around,
you tell 'em, girl!

chat with neighbor
goes on too long —
puppy starts to dig up the yard

how did those other dogs
learn to trot sweetly
alongside their humans?

every pup
looks cute
when scratching

pup multitasking:
gnaw chew stick and
hold leg up for tummy rub

puppy knows:
behind this fence lives
a big, loud, scary dog

she's above average
in number of leashes
she has bitten through

postmodern pup
deconstructs
every chew stick

puppy
pawprints
in the snow

pup in new snow
shows the world
what *frolic* means

she lowers her bottom
to pee in the snow —
look of shock!

please,
let's not eat the yellow snow,
okay?

first snow —
"okay, who redecorated
my bathroom?"

first time
in snow boots —
a comedy act

snow has messed with
all the scent cues
for where to poop

puppy's superpower:
making us
laugh

why behave,
when being destructive
gets so much attention?

"I heel crossing the street,
you give me a treat —
that's our deal, right?"

underside
presented for tummy rub —
who can resist?

Puppy Delivery Service
brings spatula
into home office

how to get pup
from A to B?
roll a ball from A to B

panic in the ant colony
when a big puppy paw
lands in their midst

she understands us —
soon we will have to
spell words

she does not chew
our phones —
doubtless just an oversight

pup tries
to herd us together
into the same room

Fetch is easy —
Drop It
is hard

I sew up the holes
that puppy's claws have torn
in our comforter

transition to big-dog food —
fine, except for
the diarrhea

no barking please,
stop barking, knock it off,
quiet! stop it! QUIET!

she lost interest
in power cords —
when will TP lose its charm?

big girls rarely have accidents,
but when they do:
big puddle

she runs back with the ball,
pounces on my thighs —
all black and blue

gently
I rub the top of her head —
I swear she's purring

switched from three to two
meals a day,
she is wildly interested in treats

how to get a pup
to calm down:
wait a few years

some day
she'll be old –
puppy time is precious

oh geez
puppy,
what now?!

Dog

Haiku

the dog and my beloved
in silhouette
on an evening walk

high school band
marches down our street —
drives the dog crazy

quiet house,
sound of dog
lapping water

every person we meet
is her new
best friend

she skids down hallway
on her belly,
otterwise

drama queen —
extravagantly
hungry, hot, tired, itchy, bored...

that clump of sod
will trigger
her intestinal engineering

under the table,
a cold nose is wedged
between my knees

wildly excited
when we get to the vet's —
she's forgotten it all

when I'm working,
she makes a pile of toys
outside the closed door

Go pee! — she bounds outside
and promptly forgets
why she's there

it's not good manners
to scooch your bottom
on their rug

aaacckkk! where on earth
did she get a can
of machinery lubricant?

tiny bit of chicken —
she licks her bowl
across the kitchen floor

we arrive home
to an ecstatic,
full-body wiggle

of course
she went through the mud,
of course she did

she sees me naked —
no judgment,
no comment

those eyes
those beautiful eyes
those great big beautiful brown eyes

the nose end must approve
before the tail end
can do its business

she counts her humans:
"one … where's two? where's two!"
crisis!!

"go for a walk?
it's ninety-two degrees!
have you lost your mind?"

a good scratching
under the chin —
her kind of bliss

she wants to be
on the other side
of any closed door

she doesn't need much —
food, walks, toys, bed, vet care,
love, grooming, treats, training …

all that is most interesting
lies just beyond the reach
of the leash

happy tail
beats jazzy rhythm
on the garbage can

opportunist
finds hole in treat bag —
later, intestinal upset

"why do you call me Sweet Girl
when we're engaged
in a fierce game of tug?"

she pulls paper
from the waste basket —
specializing in receipts

I chop carrots
in the kitchen
with an attentive companion

cat and dog eye each other —
dog is excited,
cat looks away

he calls loudly for her
as she sits quietly
behind him

dead squirrel —
so disgusting,
so exciting

overheard: *hi, sweetie! hi, girl!*
no, leave it, no! No! Leave it!
crash

dog alerts us to dangers:
kids, trucks, other dogs,
squirrels, rain, leaves

dog has horizontal speed,
but squirrel has
vertical advantage

she finds a way to press
against my body
during each yoga pose

those loud dogs
are working things out —
no need for you to get involved

how on earth
does that long tongue
fit into that small mouth?

her goal: find the midpoint
of any group of people —
occupy it

focused, excited,
nose to ground —
tracking a Yeti

push ball under couch,
then howl —
great way to get attention

am I imagining
or is she chewing
in time to the music?

hey fuzz-face —
you need to visit
the groomer

panting tongue
covered with bits
of grass

we try to sleep in —
she loudly lists all the reasons
why we should not

sticky matter in her eye —
scientific name:
gunk

her game: grab a towel,
look you in the eye,
run with it!

her nose
knows
where the treats are

I imitate her barks —
she looks at me
peculiarly

her graceful leap
onto my lap —
a kind of levitation

roasted chicken —
she stands close,
I feel her warm breath

don't jump on me
right now — I'm carrying
hot coffee

it's a big job,
monitoring the world
from the window

gooey
gluey
chew stick

today's lesson:
it's hard to fetch a ball
with a frisbee in your mouth

she's learned to pirouette —
not quite ready
for the Joffrey Ballet

dog waits outside the bathroom,
her shadow in the slit
between door and floor

all that junk hanging
from her beard —
what she has been eating

overgrown fur
highlights the waggle
in her walk

she runs a stick
along the metal fence —
each post rings

snoozing — noise! — eye opens —
worth a bark?
nah — eye closes

tongue curls upward —
she can't keep
her chin clean

I let her win at tug,
she comes right back —
play is better than win

she gallops
down the hallway
like a herd of one dog

mud-covered tongue
covers
chew toy with mud

it's hard to bark while pooping,
or is it
the other way around?

she lies on her back
just to remind us
how cute she is

no grocery bag
enters this house
without full inspection

she has no plan
for what she'll do
if she actually catches a squirrel

her sleepy eyes roll down,
only the whites
show

we understand
the plausibility of
the dog ate my homework

we walk along
at a brisk pace,
poop bag swinging

wait, you just kissed the dog
on the mouth
and now you're kissing me?

she's fierce until
neighbor stops to chat —
"belly rub?"

walks take longer
after rain —
all those interesting smells

pant pant pant, hot day,
pant pant pant
"another block? geez, mom!"

she has remarkable hearing,
except when she
doesn't want to hear

she looks
like she's been eating dirt —
she has

newly groomed,
so fluffy, so soft,
for a while

she catches popcorn —
is instantly focused
on the next one

a wet dog
smells like
a wet dog

he who pauses
in scratching her
gets a paw on his arm

run to the bedroom,
steal the underwear,
make a quick getaway

No No No
it's not polite to roll
in the neighbors' geraniums

her autumn delight —
all those
acorn-addled squirrels

where is your ball?
stunned look — "oh, I forgot!"
she races to find it

she will do anything
if you show her
kibble

noise in the kitchen —
she runs
to check it out

how to brush those teeth
when the toothpaste
is wildly exciting?

she waits
at the full length of her leash
while I pick up the poop

couples massage: together,
we nuzzle, pet and scratch
the dog

we offer treats
to distract her from the junk,
but first she eats the junk

snuffle marks
on every window
at dog level

master gaslighter:
"no, you didn't feed me dinner,
you forgot"

"postal carrier!
delivery person!
might give me a treat!"

velcro dog —
attached to you
wherever you go

utility work on our street —
the dog
is a nervous wreck

rabbit poop
looks just like kibble —
it would be rude to pass it up

nothing better than fetch,
especially when the ball
tastes good and squeaks

closet door is open
slippers!
slippers!

under the table,
dog passes gas —
everyone tries to ignore it

sly one — walks toward a stick,
then lunges left
for a mushroom

on her snout,
burrs that she pulled
off her paws

the stinkier,
the more
interesting

she barks out the window
like a cranky person
yelling at the kids

small bowl
of kibble
yields so much poop

she knows the sounds
of all the cars
in our family

talking about
vaccinations —
we cover her ears

she
loves
raw cucumber

tug
and fetch
are deeply satisfying

she rolls over, dances,
chases her tail —
all I asked was *Sit*

she travels outside for
business, reconnaissance,
pleasure

no one else around here
has eyes
as big as their nose

mouth wide open,
loud chewing, burps —
wild enjoyment of chew sticks

a paw on my arm —
"more snuggling,
please"

clean-up time —
flies object to the closing
of the poop buffet

morning is playtime,
so is afternoon,
and evening

cute little bottom
bouncing
down the stairs

so where did you get
that snootful
of dust bunnies?

no one else at this table
is getting
their bare toes washed

she comes to us
at quiet times:
"might I suggest a bit of tug?"

whatever smells that good
has got to be
disgusting

she finds
a patch of sunshine
on the cold floor

she always takes time
to stop and smell
the whatever

twenty degrees below zero,
dog is stuck inside —
booooored

she jumps up onto my lap —
well, hello there,
kibble-breath!

after a scolding,
she brings a toy —
"let's play! keep me out of trouble!"

tummy alarm goes off,
supper isn't ready —
this is serious

scratch marks on every door
that she's tried to get through —
that's all of them

there she lies,
calmly growing tangled mats
of hair

fetch turns into tug,
tug turns into fetch —
it's all pretty fluid

his perfect lawn has
Pick Up Your Poop signs —
he glares as we walk by

"ahrooooooo!"
her ball must be
under the couch again

"go pee? oh, you mean
go bark at the neighborhood —
sure, I'll do that!"

the repair guy leaves –
she races around
to let off steam

dog snuggles on my lap,
watching the birds
outside in the snow

I read too long
in her nighttime chair —
she bumps my leg with her nose

Come!
clearly means
come if there's nothing better to do

ouch!
ah, that's where she left
her cow

it's hard
to chew ferociously
when you have to pant

the gong of kibble
hitting metal bowl —
dog careens down the hallway

she licks moisture
from the windows
on cold days

snow turns
maturing dog
back into wild pup

snow banked along sidewalks —
it's like all the rest rooms
are closed

she looks up from couch
as man runs by —
"wait, did I just miss something?"

furry snout
brushes the back of my leg —
who could that be?

arctic spell —
"another walk?
what is wrong with you people?"

very cold weather —
she pees
efficiently

cute little nose —
olfactory
supercomputer

dog stretches out,
her tail thumping
the floor

new toy —
first she covers it
with slobber

can't get his attention —
she runs to the bedroom
to get his socks

we get her to stop barking,
she gives one last
disgruntled woof

after a nap,
her fuzzy face
is cockeyed flat on one side

no one does anything
in the kitchen
without an audience

fuzzy snuffles
on my toes
in the morning

151

her feathery tail
swishes the dust
in the air

dog
wants in
on all family hugs

she looks up at me,
head cocked,
mouth full of ball

C'mon, let's go for a walk!
sleepy dog:
"better idea — let's not"

bathroom door doesn't latch —
she noses it open —
now we're both in here

warm dog
warm lap
warm heart

she's our sweet pooch,
our crazy mutt,
our baby

what was life like
before we had this dog?
I don't remember

she still
pulls
the toilet paper

Author's Note

Readers will note that most of these haiku do not follow the familiar 5-7-5 syllable pattern. I refer readers to Billy Collins's "Introduction" in *Haiku in English: The First Hundred Years* (edited by Kacian, Rowland and Burns) and the "Foreword to the Third Edition" of *The Haiku Anthology* by editor Cor van den Heuvel. Both dismiss the strict syllabic convention. Like Billy Collins, however, I do find an overall limit of 17 syllables per haiku to be a useful levee against any potential overflow of words.

I am aware that some of the entries in *What Now?!* will not be considered haiku or senryu by those who are knowledgeable about haiku and senryu. Actually, I agree, so let's not squabble.

In whatever form and by whatever name, these entries were written to capture the whimsy and delight in our moment-by-moment experiences with our beloved Poppy.

About the Author

Melissa S. Anderson and her beloved husband live in Minneapolis, Minnesota, with their dog, Poppy (see cover photos). Melissa is an artist, poet and mystic. She spent 36 years at the University of Minnesota, where she was a professor of higher education, and five years teaching in the math department at St. Olaf College earlier in her career. Her book, ***Prof Notes: Wry Observations on Academic Life***, is based on her years at the University.

What Now?! and ***Prof Notes*** can be ordered through your favorite bookstore. Print and e-book versions are also available at Barnes & Noble and Amazon.

Check Melissa's website for more information and other options for ordering:

mandwriter.com